True North Quest
Reflection Journal

WAYNE & GABRIELLE ENRIGHT

Wayne & Gabrielle Enright wish to pay respect to Elders past and present, and to acknowledge the Traditional Owners of the lands upon which our journeys take place.

Published 2018 by Wayne & Gabrielle Enright

ISBN: 978-0-6483899-0-3 (Spiral Bound)
         978-0-6483899-1-0 (EPub)
         978-0-6483899-2-7 (Paperback)
         978-0-6483899-3-4 (Hardback)
Topic: Personal Growth and Leadership Development

All Rights Reserved
Copyright © 2018 Wayne & Gabrielle Enright

This work is copyright and may not be reproduced without the written consent of the authors, in accordance with the Australian Copyright Act 1968. To seek consent or to order hard copies, please contact: wayne@freespirittruenorth.com.au

Printed by: Openbook Howden Print and Design, St Marys, South Australia

Disclaimers:
The material in this publication is of a general nature, expressed as opinion by the authors and does not represent professional advice. It is not intended to provide specific guidance for any individual or organisation and should not be relied upon as such. Readers should seek professional advice on matters pertaining to their personal circumstances. The authors accept no responsibility or liability for the use or misuse of information in this publication.

The authors are solely responsible for the choice and presentation of the contents of this book and for the opinions expressed therein.

Contents

Introduction 1
A Compass for Life, Learning and Leadership 1
The Spirit of Adventure Calls 2
Experiential Learning Cycle 3
The Quest for True North 6
Opening the Awareness Window 8

The New Frontier 11
Brave New World 11
New Frontier Leadership 13
Seeking a Mentor 15

True North Leadership Compass 16
A Compass for New Frontier Leaders 16
The Spiral Journey 17
Mentors, Milestones and Sacred Places 17
The Four Directions 23

Finding True North 25
Your Medicine 29
Integrity 32
Authenticity 34
Navigating Life 37

Resilience 49
Emotional Intelligence 50
Patience and Persistence 50
Failing your Way to Success 51
Developing Emotional Resilience 53
Living your Best Life 54
Surfing the Balance Zone 55
The Gift of Illness 56
Surviving to Thriving 58
Transcendence and the Trans-personal 60

Responsibility 62
Responding to Change and Challenge 62
The Mindfulness Paradox 63
Living in Present Time 63
Breathe without Judgement 65
Self-mastery and Life Balance 67

Influence 69
Earning the Right to Lead 69
Social Intelligence 70
Empathy and Diversity 71
Understanding 72
Constructive Conflict 75
Non-judgement 76
The Gift of Feedback 76
Embracing Differences 78

The Ripple Effect 81
The Myth of Self-Mastery 83
Challenging the Inner Rules 85
From Story to Possibility 85
Fear Guards our Most Valuable Treasure 86

Appendices 89
   1. Animal Instincts Profile 90
   2. Emotional Intelligence Profile 91
   3. Intention and Commitments 92
   4. Circle of Stones 93
   5. Dream Arrow 95
   6. Creed Beads 95
   7. Vision Board 96
   8. Gratitude List 96

*Within all journeys are hidden gems of immense value.
These treasures remain unknown unless we search for them.
Sometimes we half-hear them in the stillness of a forest,
at sunset or between two waves in an ocean of noise.
Reflection is the key to discovery.*

Introduction

A Compass for Life, Learning and Leadership
Our world shall never be well understood by theory alone, life experience is much more valuable. Although the journey of personal growth requires each of us to explore and find our own path, it is surely of great use to a young person, before they set out on their journey through a life full of twists and turns, mountains and mazes, to at least have a map and compass to guide them, made by an experienced traveller.

Inspired by
The Letters of the Earl of Chesterfield to His Son.

This journal is a companion to the publication: *The Spirit of Adventure Calls – A Compass for Life, Learning and Leadership.* We trust that it will serve as a helpful guide that will lead you to your own True North – the place in this world where you live in alignment with your purpose, speak your truth and exist with more ease and grace, despite life's inevitable challenges.

May you find among these pages, a sacred place to reflect on your journey as you explore your vision, your values, your gifts, passions and strengths. Your most powerful 'Medicine' will be to discover these things and share them with others. As you do this, you will develop a stronger sense of who you are and why you are here. Every life has a sacred purpose, a 'True North' – the quest to find it can lead to many other valuable discoveries along the way.

Please note: References to Figures, Page Numbers and Chapters in this journal will lead you to the relevant sections of *The Spirit of Adventure Calls* publication, where you can read stories and further information.

The Spirit of Adventure Calls
Where does a person go to learn their soul's name—a name that defines their true identity? Obtaining this deep heart wisdom may require us to undergo a process of initiation. To discover the truth of who we are, we often need to take a journey that challenges us.

Our modern world is full of uninitiated people. Knowledge is taught in classrooms but for many there is a lack of rites of passage or opportunities to face the challenges of the wilder side of life in the presence of wise elders. Emotional Intelligence is not learnt in classrooms but in the experience of living life's challenges, joys and lessons of the heart.

Adventuring into unknown territory takes us out of our comfort zone and into the learning zone, where we have the opportunity to test our inner resources, challenge the inner rules we live by and discover the universe of our potential.

"Adventure is not about conquering nature. It is about the journey within us that takes place when we explore the frontiers of our personal boundaries, taking ourselves to places we normally wouldn't venture to go, and then returning to lead a richer, more colourful life because of our experience! When the spirit of adventure calls to our heart, we must go."

Figure 14.2 **The Experiential Learning Cycle**—adapted from Kolb45 & Lewin, 1990

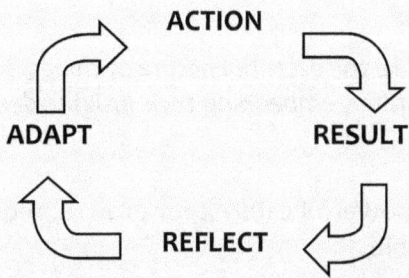

1. **ACTION**
   The learner takes action, trying out the strategies and processes in his or her current *action theory*. (This can happen consciously but is most often done unconsciously.)

2. **RESULT**
   The learner then experiences the consequences/results of their actions. Results usually provide feedback about whether one's actions are helpful or not, but it is not always a given that the learner will notice a *teachable moment*. The learner needs to consciously look for the feedback inherent in the results of their actions or have their attention drawn to it by a facilitator.

3. **REFLECT** (Lewin combines *Stages 2 and 3*)
   Feedback can be from the experience itself (success/failure) or from others observing and interacting with participants. It can also come from self-reflection. In most facilitated programs, the facilitator will provide participants with some specific reflection questions which lead to insights about behaviour and results. Thus the learner discovers what works and what doesn't.

4. **ADAPT** (Lewin labels this as the *Integration* Stage)
   As a result of this process of feedback, examination and reflection on the consequences of their actions, the learner integrates this updated information and experience into a new *action theory*, thus adapting their behaviour for new situations.

   It is the last two stages that make the difference between having a learning experience or just having an experience without learning.

Adventure-Based Experiential Learning
Adventure can be used as a potent learning and development tool, providing opportunities to learn through the metaphors inherent in adventure and nature. Metaphor conveys a level of understanding that is beyond the rational, linear thinking mind.

> *Metaphor and myth capture the essential nature of things, somehow by-passing the brain's logical filter, embedding their insights deep within us.*

Adventure can thus be a powerful catalyst for growth, requiring more from us than we might think possible.

It challenges our self-belief, our resilience, courage and strength of character. Although we may feel discomfort and fear; on a deeper level we yearn to know that we have what it takes to meet adventure's test.

When was the last time you experienced something adventurous where you were challenged either physically, mentally, emotionally, socially and/or spiritually?

(Where, when, what happened, what did you learn, how did it change you?)

The Quest for True North
A quest can be defined as a journey taken in the pursuit of answers to important questions or a mission to discover knowledge, wisdom or valuable treasure. The objective of a quest is often hidden and often requires one to overcome challenges along the way. Challenges provide an initiation of sorts, developing within us a strength and wisdom that we weren't necessarily seeking. It is not what we achieve at the end of our quest that is most important, but what we learn and who we become along the way. The quest for True North is thus a rite of passage that initiates us into the truth of who we are and helps us to discover our true purpose in life.

> *"All journeys have secret destinations
> of which the traveller is unaware."*
> Martin Buber

Reflecting on your life so far...
What unexpected challenges, blessings, meetings, experiences, lessons (secret destinations); have you discovered along the way?

What do you desire to know, understand, learn, experience, achieve or let go of during your quest?

(Describe some of the niggling questions that remain unanswered)

Figure 15.1 **Awareness Window**, adapted Johari Window—Luft & Ingham, 1955

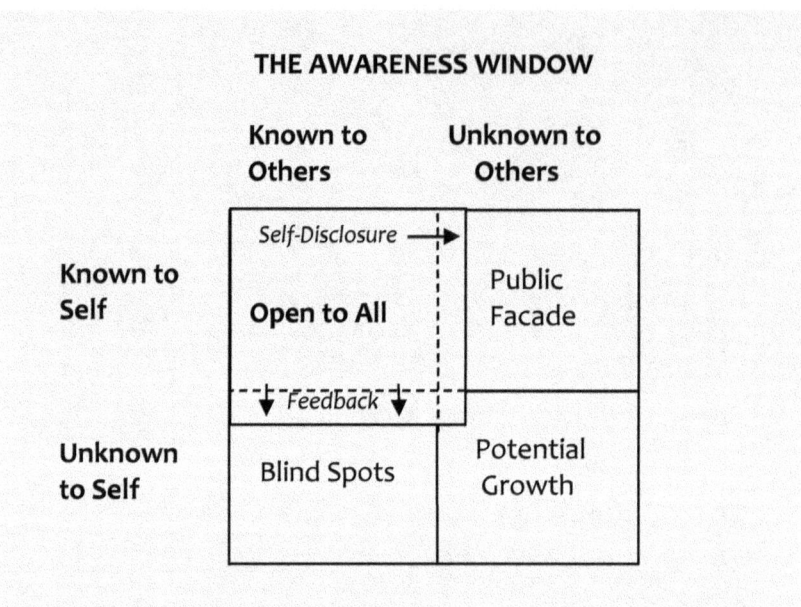

Opening the Awareness Window
Each of us has an 'Awareness Window' through which we understand ourself and others. Our view through this window is influenced by how well we know ourselves, our willingness to share our true self and our openness to feedback from others and from our life experiences.

Experiential learning journeys help us to open up this window, thus revealing the attitudes and behaviours that help or hinder our relationships and performance. Becoming aware of our 'blindspots' helps us to grow.

How often do you take time out to reflect on what you are learning and how you can improve the way you live your life?

When and where would be a good time and place to make space for personal reflection?

Who are those in your life that you respect and trust enough to seek feedback from?

What 'blindspots' (strengths or areas for improvement) **have you discovered so far by experience and/or feedback from others?**

The New Frontier

Brave New World

The world's social and economic landscape has dramatically changed since the mid 1900s. We've experienced an explosion of consumerism, the social revolution of the 60s, the formation of networks and alliances and the booming information age. We now operate in a highly competitive global marketplace where rapid communication speeds up interactions, resulting in the need for flatter structures that are more responsive and adaptable.

This brave new world requires us to be more resilient, adaptable and open to continuous learning. Many of the top performing organisations globally, agree that the characteristics most wanted in employees are not intellectual or technical expertise, but their ability to work in teams, having great communication skills, a passion for learning and a real enjoyment of change.

> *"It is not necessarily the strongest that survive,*
> *it is the most adaptable"*
> Charles Darwin

What strengths do you already have that will help you adapt to this brave new world?

What characteristics would you like to develop further to help you thrive in this brave new world?

_____
_____
_____
_____
_____
_____
_____
_____
_____

What action could you take to assist your personal or professional development in these areas?

_____
_____
_____
_____
_____
_____
_____
_____
_____

New Frontier Leadership
Workers in this more chaotic and fast moving environment need to be able to make self-directed decisions without having to wait for an answer from above before they can make a move. Therefore the type of leadership necessary to survive and indeed thrive in this new frontier is completely different.

The environment we now live and work in calls for a new approach to leadership which we refer to as the 'New Leadership Frontier'. The new frontier challenges old models of leadership which can become a liability in this new world context. New frontier leaders need to be more authentic, courageous, resilient and creative.

Successful organisations that embrace these new needs for team and leadership development will be more focused on learning outcomes such as emotional intelligence development, resilience building, innovative thinking and principle-centered decision making.

Figure 20.2 **The Journey to Self-Management**—Adapted from G Donovan, 2001

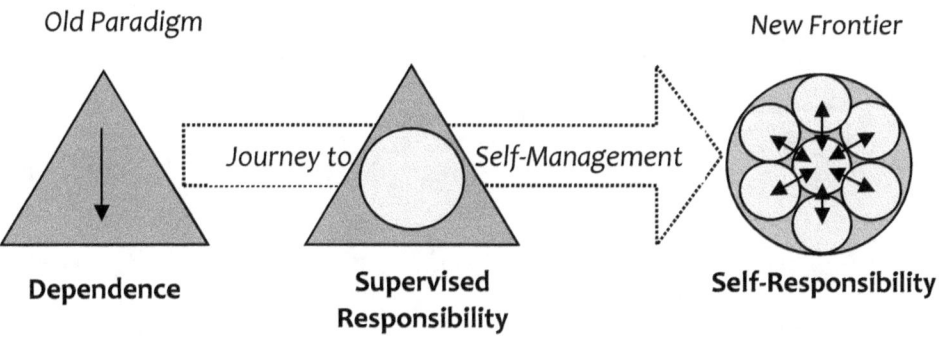

*Living and working in the new frontier will require us
to be more self-directed, adaptable, rapid learners
with strong emotional and social intelligence.*

Choose one or two people that you look up to as a leadership role model? (you may or may not know them personally).

_____
_____
_____
_____
_____
_____
_____

What character traits do they have that you see in yourself or would like to develop? (alongside each trait, indicate which are your strengths or areas for development)

_____
_____
_____
_____
_____
_____
_____
_____
_____

Seeking a Mentor

A mentor is a person, like a coach or counsellor, who you respect and trust that can help you learn and improve personally and/or professionally. They are usually a person who is already where you'd like to be and has the experience to guide you. Mentors don't necessarily just give advice, they teach with questions, stories, being an empathic sounding board and encourager. Although they are a reliable supporter, they may also challenge you from time to time.

You can have mentors for different aspects of your life, whether it be finances, relationships, handling stress or to help you with your physical, mental or spiritual health. Finding a mentor who you relate to as an honest and trusted guide is one of the greatest blessings in life.

*A true master is not the one with the most students
but the one who develops the most masters.*

Who would/could you choose as a mentor to help you become the leader you would like to be (e.g. as a student, parent, on the sports field, in your community, family or at work)?

_____

_____

_____

_____

_____

_____

_____

_____

_____

True North Leadership Compass

Figure 26.1 **The True North Leadership Compass**—W&G Enright © 2014

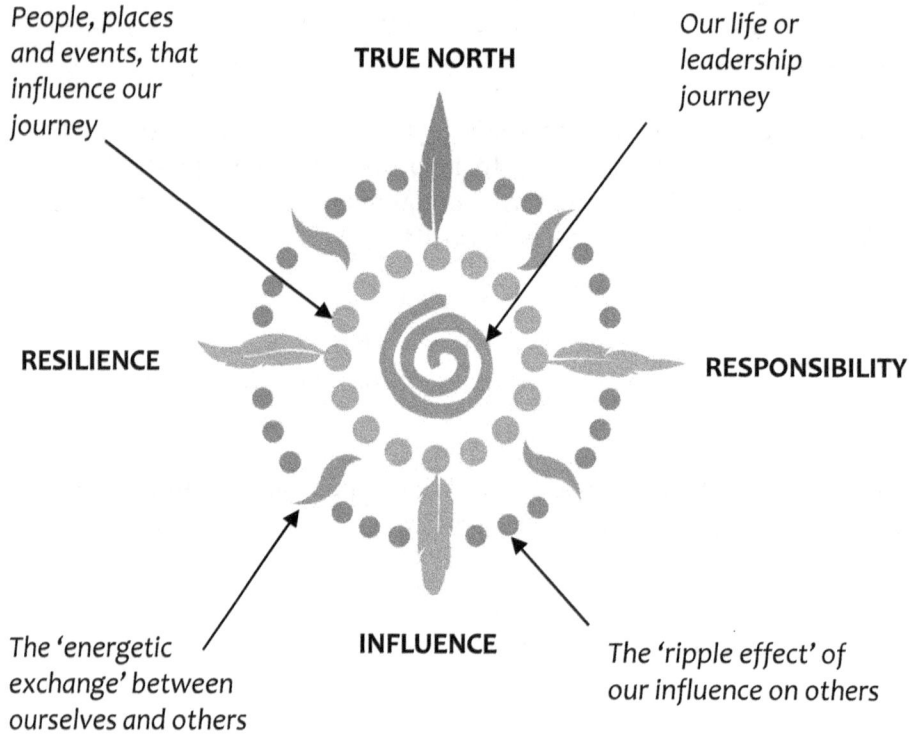

A Compass for New Frontier Leaders

The True North Leadership Compass is a valuable model for new frontier leaders or anyone who would like to take charge of their own life and make difference in the world, regardless of whether they're in a formal position of leadership or not. Leadership is not about position or title, it is about character and is defined by your attitude and behaviour in relationships with others.

The True North Leadership compass framework helps us to see our journey as a continuous process of growth, to have gratitude for the mentors, milestones and sacred places that have shaped us, and to identify our strengths and areas for development.

The Spiral Journey
The spiral represents the journey we all take in life as we revisit questions we thought we had answered, lessons we thought we had learned and challenges we thought we had overcome. We transform as we travel a continuous orbit around the sun of our life, revisiting familiar challenges but from a place of ever-evolving maturity like the rings of a tree.

Our life journey is a never-ending spiral of experiences which provide us with an opportunity to build on the lessons from the past and evolve into our future potential.

Mentors, Milestones and Sacred Places
The circles of influence that surround the spiral symbolise the people, places and events that impact our life journey and therefore our development as a person. They influence our values, our beliefs, our character, and the development of our knowledge and skills. These defining influences often help us to find our True North.

*"Be grateful for the times that almost break you,
and always remember those who shaped you."*

Inspired by Sarah Haze

Mentors

Who have been the most influential people in your life?
Describe what you have learned from them.

Milestones

Draw a 'life line' down the left side of the next page or two and divide it into sections to represent the years of your life so far. Then mark on the line: your most significant learning experiences, turning points or defining moments.

There is valuable treasure buried within the defining experiences of our Spiral Journey. On the quest to find True North we can ask the question:

What have I learnt from the triumphs and tragedies that are sprinkled throughout my life story and how have they shaped me?

Sacred Places

What are the most memorable places that you've been and which places do you hold most sacred? (What is special for you about each place?)

The Four Directions

1. **True North**
2. **Responsibility**
3. **Resilience**
4. **Influence**

The four directions of the compass are character traits or skills that can be developed over time. Our level of awareness, confidence, competence and commitment in these four areas will help us to be more effective in life generally and particularly when it comes to leading or influencing others constructively.

What would be your initial assessment of yourself for each of these four aspects of life and leadership skills?

Circle the rating you would give yourself and highlight or underline key words in the description to indicate areas for improvement in your awareness, confidence, skill or level of commitment.

Rating Scale

1 = Limited awareness, skill or commitment in this area. A significant area for development.

5 = Some level of competence in this are but not as confident or consistent as I'd like to be.

10 = I feel very confident and competent in this area of the compass.

True North
The ability to stay true to your mission, vision, and values while navigating your way through conflicting priorities, unexpected pressures, ethical dilemmas and tensions between your head and your heart. It is about living and speaking your truth, being authentic and acting always with integrity.

1   2   3   4   5   6   7   8   9   10

Resilience
The ability to regulate your emotions when you are challenged; the level of patience and persistence you bring to the fore when things don't go to plan; your tolerance for failure and your ability to withstand sustained pressure or multiple setbacks.

1   2   3   4   5   6   7   8   9   10

Responsibility
The ability to stay calm and respond mindfully to change and challenges. Being able to learn and adapt by reflecting on the lessons from adversity. Finding innovative solutions to problems and having the courage to take risks.

1   2   3   4   5   6   7   8   9   10

Influence
The ability to inspire, encourage and empower others, thus multiplying your influence. The level of empathy, humility, trust, honesty and respect you have for others. Your ability to communicate, negotiate and manage conflict constructively.

1   2   3   4   5   6   7   8   9   10

"Only the brave should lead, those whose integrity cannot be shaken, whose minds are enlightened enough to understand the high calling of the leader."

Adapted from Pearl S Buck

Finding True North

True North is often used as a metaphor for the concept of integrity and authenticity (alignment with personal values, beliefs, truth) because it is seen as constant and 'true' compared with magnetic north which varies and is dependent on where you are. The direction of north on a compass may also be influenced by its surroundings if you hold it close to a metal belt buckle or fence post. We too can be affected by the energy of those around us. It is harder to live one's truth in the absence of an inner compass.

So, True North can be thought of in terms of our inner guidance system—a way of living that is most aligned with what we feel is our true mission in life. Many of us wander through life following the direction of someone else's compass or with no compass at all. Some of us find a compass later in life which points us in the right direction. Whatever the timing, eventually we must find for ourselves, the truth of who we are and follow our own inner guidance if we are to feel fulfilled and well within. This is the essence of what it means to live and lead with authenticity and integrity. Finding and following one's True North is one of the most pivotal challenges of leadership and in the grander scheme of life.

True North is not only about our values, beliefs and sense of true-self, it is also about the vision we hold for ourselves, and how we use our gifts to live a meaningful life. Sometimes discovering this requires us to let go of the past and embrace the future.

What guiding principles do you live by?
(Values that for you are non-negotiable and that guide your decision making and behavior)

Achievement	Respect	Efficiency	Compassion
Accuracy	Tidyness	Bravery	Love
Being Organised	Forgiveness	Fun	Responsibility
Doing My Best	Risk-taking	Service	Winning
Clear Communication	Honesty	Creativity	Balance
Learning	Integrity	Control	Perfection
Sacrifice	Kindness	Consideration	Fairness
Approval	Punctuality	Patience	Authenticity

You may like to select from the list of values above or come up with some of your own.

What would be your Top 4 Values?
These can become a useful compass for decision-making!

_____
_____
_____
_____
_____
_____

Purpose
Our purpose in life is often not clear to us until later in life if ever. It doesn't have to be grandiose or unique necessarily. It could be to be a gardener, a handyman or cleaner. These may not seem like 'world famous' vocations but each of them can contribute significantly to the quality of life of others. A purpose doesn't even have to be a vocation, it could just be the gift of listening to another, sharing art or being a loving parent, brother or sister. As long as we follow the path of our happiness, follow our bliss, and live from the heart, this will usually lead us to where we need to be.

*Be aware of that which has meaning for you
and let it be your guide.
Live your truth with kindness and authenticity and let it be
a compass for your journey through life.*

**Do you have an inkling of your purpose?
What might it be?**

Describe the vision you hold for your life.

What is your 'Medicine' (Your unique gifts and talents)?
In North-American indigenous cultures, the word 'Medicine' is sometimes used to refer to the unique gifts and talents that you bring to the world in the service of others and the planet.

(Even if we are not yet aware of how to use them, they can be our most powerful medicine for healing or empowering ourselves and those we share them with.)

What are some of the possible ways you can share your 'medicine' for the benefit of others or our planet?

To feel the love of family,
to love, to laugh, to climb a tree.
To sing, to run, to swim in the sea.
To walk in Nature's beauty to see
the vistas, the life, the energy.
To give to others and know they are me.
These are the things that set my heart free.

WB Enright

What sets your heart free?

Where and when do you feel most alive to your true nature?

Integrity
The first person we must learn to lead is ourselves. We need to have our own act together, including our ability to make good decisions in critical situations; to trust ourselves; to have integrity when others try to push us out of shape; and to be authentic despite sometimes being pressured by the world to be someone other than our true self. Integrity, authenticity, honesty and respect are the hallmarks of a reliable and trustworthy character.

Having the courage to live by and stand up for our values is the essence of integrity. Integrity literally means having 'wholeness of character.' Doing the 'right thing' in a consistent and reliable way is a character trait that people admire, because it means a person has a moral compass that doesn't waver. Integrity is based on one's strength of character and the ability to withstand pressure from outside forces.

"If you stand for nothing, you'll fall for anything."

It is particularly impressive to see young people who are able to speak their truth and live in alignment with their moral compass in the midst of powerful peer group pressure. It takes courage to be different and stand up for what you believe in.

"To be yourself in a world that is constantly trying to make you something else, is the greatest accomplishment."

Ralph Waldo Emerson

When do you find it most challenging to stay true to your values?
(What are some of the pressures/challenges of life that can make it difficult?)

What intention could you set for yourself, that would reinforce your personal integrity? (Who could support you with this commitment to yourself?)

Authenticity
Being authentic is a major pillar of integrity and relies on us being self-aware enough to know our true self and brave enough to live in alignment with it. Knowing who we are, what we stand for and having the courage to follow our truth and live by our values, does not mean that we can't be flexible or be influenced by the feedback or needs of others. If we need to do this, we can do it consciously and in ways that do not compromise our principles.

Being authentic involves sharing more of who we truly are. Authenticity will usually enable a leader to build greater affinity, trust and engagement with those they lead, but only if their authenticity is relatable, respectful and adaptable to the needs of others. It is a mistake to use authenticity as an excuse for being a rude and arrogant bully or someone who uses humour as a put down. It always comes back to our intention in any given moment.
It is helpful to be conscious of our intentions or to reflect on our sub-conscious intentions when we do something that might be 'out of character.'

The challenge of leadership
is to be strong but not rude;
kind but not weak;
bold but not bully;
thoughtful but not lazy;
humble but not timid;
proud but not arrogant;
have humour but without folly.

Jim Rohn

What are some of the things we can do to make it easier for ourselves and others to express our authentic selves?

Our deepest fear is not that we are inadequate. Our deepest fear is that we are powerful beyond measure. It is our light, not our darkness that most frightens us. We ask ourselves, Who am I to be brilliant, gorgeous, talented, and fabulous? Actually, who are you not to be? Your playing small does not serve the world. We are all meant to shine and as we let our own light shine, we give others permission to do the same. As we are liberated from our own fear, our presence liberates others.

Abbreviated quote - Marianne Williamson
A Course in Miracles

We are all works of art
Our personality traits, values, vulnerabilities, competencies and strengths are not set in stone. Like a wise artisan, life carves away at our façade, eventually revealing the truth of who we are. We are constantly evolving, becoming aware of our blind spots and discovering strengths yet to be developed. All of us, especially leaders, are a work in progress.

Those who dare to lead
must never cease to learn and improve.

Speaking your truth
We all have a voice but many of us neglect to use it to speak our truth. We often find our true voice when we have the courage to speak up. Beneath the fear of expressing one's truth lies a powerful and authentic voice waiting to emerge.

"The key to leading with authenticity and courage,
is speaking from the heart, even when your voice shakes."
Elizabeth Powell

Respecting our authentic heart
Finding True North - the place within us which is consistent, reliable, honest and true to our values - helps us to be in a stronger position to live in alignment with our true self. It is then a question of being resilient enough to resist the forces around us that take us away from our authentic heart?

When we have the courage to speak our heart's truth
and respect the truth in the hearts of others,
peace will be inevitable.

Navigating Life

In the same way that organisations have strategic plans that define their mission, vision, values and a plan for achieving their organisational priorities; we as individuals or as a family, can also create a strategic plan for our life. Once we have clarified the direction we want to go in life and identified our desired destinations, the next step is to plan a path to our dreams.

In much the same way as you might use a map and compass to navigate your way through the wilderness, it is helpful to assess your current position, to identify the resources you'll need, and plot your course with checkpoints to review progress along the way. Being well prepared for the journey is crucial to success.

Your personal values can serve as a reliable compass to keep you on track, as you negotiate unexpected obstacles, detours and crossroads along the way.

One of the first steps in developing a navigation plan for any stage of life, is to take stock of where you currently are on the map so to speak: identify your strengths, development needs, opportunities and potential challenges.

If you fail to plan, you plan to fail

Figure 31.5 **Strategic Planning Map**—W Enright © 2004

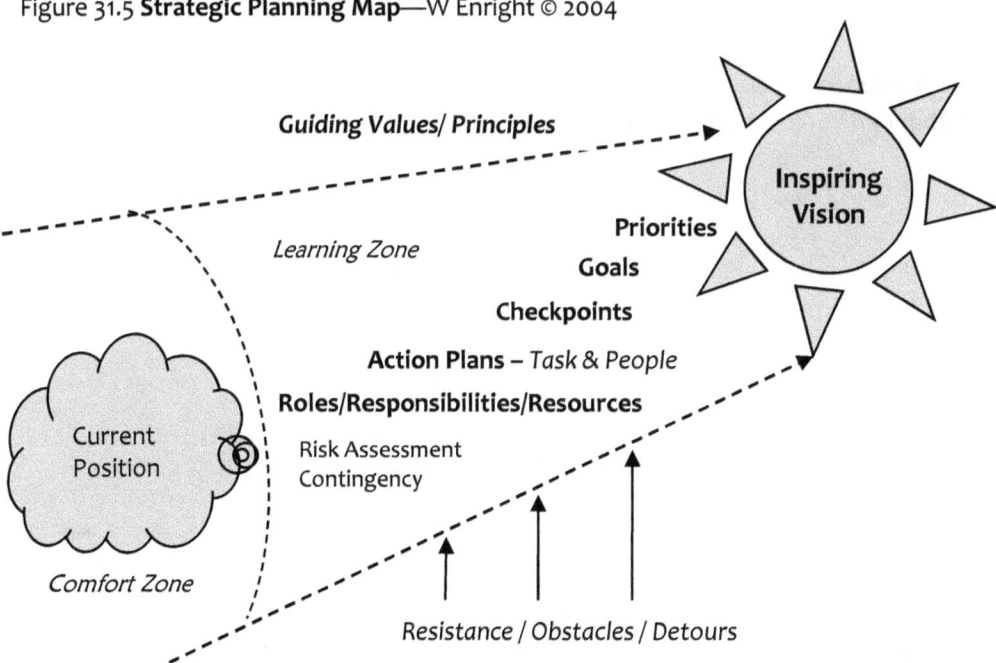

Steps for navigating life

1. **Take SDOC of where you are and identify growth priorities:**

Strengths
(How can you use them to your advantage?)

_____
_____
_____
_____
_____
_____
_____

Development needs
(What can you do to develop yourself?)

_____
_____
_____
_____
_____
_____
_____

Opportunities
(What action can you take to make the best of opportunities?)

Challenges
(What are some possible solutions to potential challenges?)

2. Create an inspiring vision

Having an inspiring vision of how we'd like our life to be, has a magical power that draws our dreams towards us. A vision needs to be inspiring enough to 'pull' you towards it, like a rubber band pulling you out of your comfort zone into the growth zone. If your vision is not strong enough, you'll be pulled back into the 'gravitational field' of your comfort zone.

Most of our limits are not set in concrete but conditioned into us by the circumstances of our past. To 'dream' is to step boldly into the realm of possibility and break free from our self-imposed limitations. It starts with lifting the lid off the boxes we put ourselves in and asking the questions - If I had the power to create the life of my own choosing, **what would I like to:**

> **HAVE**

➢ **DO**

➢ **GIVE**

- **BE: What person would I like to Become?**
  (We are human **beings** - therefore one could argue that it is more important to know how you would like to **BE**, than what you would like to DO in life).

What am I most PASSIONATE about?

In what ways is my life already aligned with my dreams and passions?

In what other ways could I create more alignment between my dreams and passions and the way I live?

*Creating a Vision Board** can be a powerful way of capturing your dreams so you can visualise them daily. (See Appendix 7)

3. Identify Specific Intentions – using SMART Goals

Tangible goals serve as checkpoints on your map and as a measure of progress. When you have completed most of the reflection questions in this journal, you'll have plenty of food for thought that will help you to develop some very clear intentions and commitments. Without clear intention and commitment knowledge has little power.

Refer to the appendix for a template you can use to set intentions in different areas of your life and to map out a personal action plan. **The SMART Goal formula** will increase your likelihood of success.

Specific

Measurable

Achievable

Responsible

Time defined.

4. Failure is an Option

Planning should always include some thinking and discussion about challenges, risks and worst-case scenarios. This can lead to useful **contingency plans** so that we are less reactive when things don't go as expected. It is helpful to **view setbacks as temporary events** that offer opportunities to learn and improve. **Identifying potential risks and challenges** to your plan, helps you to also find creative solutions when you are not under pressure.

*Write your goals in concrete
and your plans in sand*

Prioritising
Take time at the end of each day or at the beginning of the next, to write down a 'To Do' list and tick off the things completed. This provides a sense of achievement and will help you to stay on track with your priorities. Chances are there will be a number of unexpected tasks to do in addition to those tasks on your 'To Do' list which can send you in to time and energy debt. Often this can result in the neglect of other priorities such as relationships, health, time for planning, admin and learning etc.

Focus Management
In reality there is no such thing as time management; we can't really manage time, only what we do with it. The best we can do is manage our focus which is why it is important to be clear about our priorities. Investing time in thinking about what is really important to us in life and clearly defining our priorities based on our purpose and values, will make decision making much easier.

Using a Priority Map
The Priority Map (see Figure 31.7), provides a guide for prioritising your focus, and allowing time for selfcare, relationships, planning and learning.

You can reduce 'time-debt' by deleting 'time-wasters' in Quadrant D and improving responses to unexpected urgencies in Quadrant C from a mindset of choice. The 4Ds at the centre of the map, can help you to make more mindful choices when interruptions pop up, rather than react with urgency to everything.

Savings of time, money and energy can then be re-invested into building assets/strengths in Quadrant B. The 'return on investment' will help you to be happier, healthier and more productive in Quadrant A. These principles can be applied to time, money and energy.

Use the Priority Map to record 'To Do' lists in Quadrants A & B. Take note of where your time goes in Quandrant C & D during the day or week, then make some adjustments. Mapping your time, money and energy expenditure, increases self-awareness.

Figure 31.7 **Priority Map**—Enright © 2005

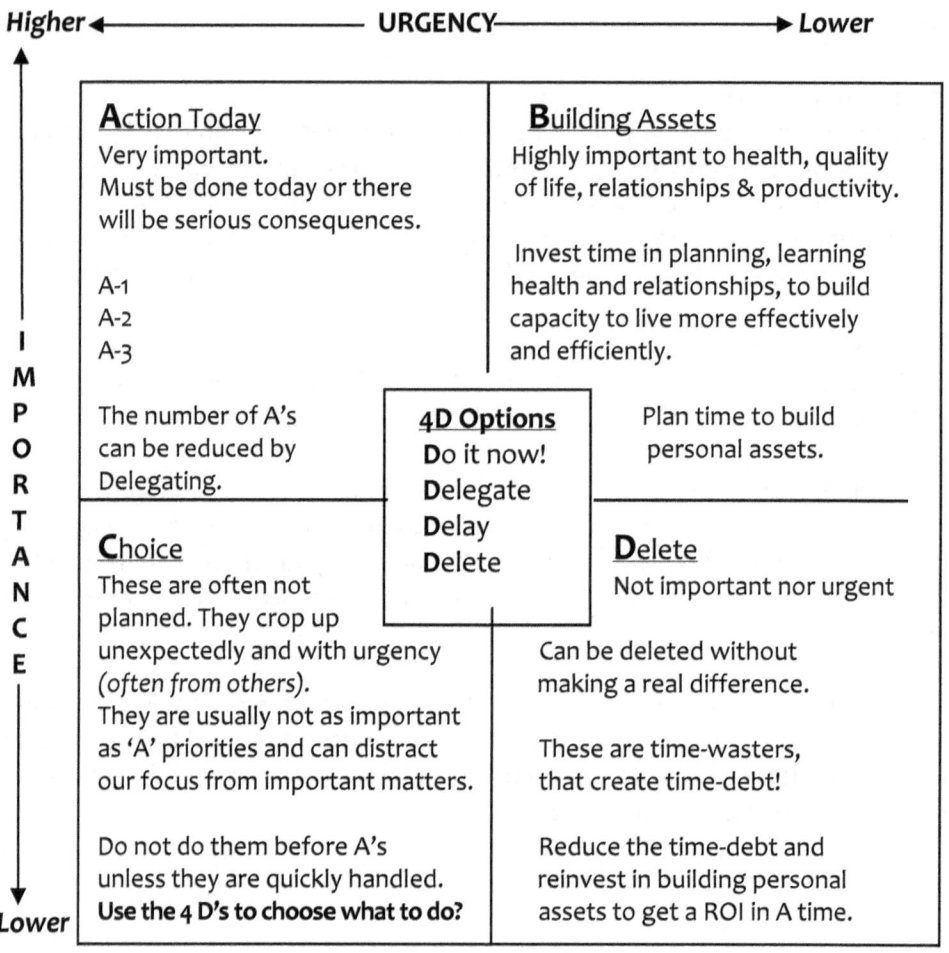

Note: You can create copies of a blank map for daily use.

Resilience

So, we've defined our True North and sorted our priorities around our purpose and values, providing us with a map and compass to guide us toward our inspiring vision. The real challenge begins when we take off on our journey toward our dreams and find that it is perhaps more challenging than we expected. This is where the rubber meets the road, and where our resilience is tested. Will our tyres be durable enough to last the distance, or will we end up on the side of the road despondently holding our map, as we search deep within ourselves for the inner resources to get us to our desired destination. This is where we discover our resilience!

Resilience is not about being tough, it's about having deep and strong foundations that give us the flexibility to adapt and grow in response to our environment like the tallest of trees that has enough flexibility to bend in gale-force winds without breaking and possesses the patience and persistence required to grow in the most adverse conditions.

In the midst of fire, I remind myself that it is actually a light that God sent to enlighten my way - to evolve, to grow and actualise my true self and become a better human being.
I now understand that life happens for me, not to me and that it is always for a reason and purpose that serves me.

Alame Leadership

Emotional Intelligence
Our ability to remain calm under pressure and choose our response rather than reacting, is somewhat determined by our emotional intelligence. One of the hallmarks of 'emotional intelligence' is the ability to maintain one's composure and positivity when things don't go the way one expects. It is normal to have an initial 'grief reaction' such as shock, disbelief frustration, disappointment, anger or sadness when things go wrong, but when we get stuck in these feelings and they inhibit our ability to respond with solutions or acceptance, we can become a victim of our emotions.

Staying calm under pressure comes naturally to some, and for others it can be more challenging. The key skill is to be mindful of our reactions when they occur and be able to regulate our emotions enough to reflect on the lessons our challenges bring. We can then grow from adversity, rather than be defeated by it.

> *"You must learn to be still in the midst of activity*
> *and vibrantly alive in repose."*
>
> Indira Gandhi

Patience and Persistence pays off
One of the most common characteristics of successful people is their ability to persist in the face of adversity—to have patience when life's timing does not align with theirs. Goals and plans often set us up for the challenge of dealing with 'failure' if we are not flexible enough to deal with the mis-match between our expectations and life's reality. If we try to force things, pushing against the flow, and allow our impatience to fill us with desperation and frustration, we can be left exhausted, frustrated and stressed to the point of giving up.

> *The river is patient, flexible and persistent*
> *the rock is rigid and unforgiving.*
> *In the struggle between the river and the rock,*
> *the river will always win,*
> *not by strength and power, but by perseverance.*
>
> Inspired by a Zen Proverb

Failing our Way to Success
People who have a higher tolerance for failure often 'fail their way to success.' Thomas Edison was a notable example. Even though his teachers said he was too stupid to learn anything he became the inventor of one of the most life changing technologies of our age. Edison made 1,000 unsuccessful attempts at inventing the electric light bulb. When a reporter asked, *"How did it feel to fail 1,000 times?"* Edison replied, *"I didn't fail 1,000 times. The light bulb was an invention with 1,000 steps."*

Apparent setbacks often lead to learning or to the planting of seeds that bear fruit after a harsh winter. Learning from failure is a key ingredient of success, nothing teaches like experience. Mountaineers, marathon runners, writers, artists and gardeners are just a few who know this truth; that setbacks are part of any worthwhile endeavour. The seeds of greatness are planted long before they bear fruit and often require a long period of focused effort sprinkled with failure, obstacles and unexpected circumstances.

> *Adversity is where grace and suffering meet to transform us.*
> *Every scar has a story to tell of pain and blessing.*

As you reflect on your 'life line' penned earlier in this quest journal – identify a couple of key moments when you experienced discouragement, that later became blessings or gifts in your life once you had moved beyond the disappointment.

How might the understanding of this assist you when faced with future disappointments?

Developing Emotional Resilience

Stress and change are essential elements of what it means to be alive and yet most people try to avoid them, staying within their comfort zone or a predictable range of outcomes. The reality is that we actually need stress and change to stimulate our body, mind and our emotions. Stress helps us grow in much the same way as a tree is strengthened by the wind. If we substitute the word 'challenge' for the word 'stress,' this helps us to think about stress as something more constructive. An optimal level of challenge strengthens us; helps us to be motivated, stimulated and fulfilled; and ultimately causes us to grow.

To identify your strengths and under-developed areas of emotional intelligence – complete the Emotional Intelligence Profile in Appendix 2: You can then use challenges as learning and growth opportunities, times when you can practice new skills such as mindfulness, conflict resolution, communication, negotiation, patience, focus management, self-reflection. With practice these skills become habitual.

Once you have completed the profile, summarise your strengths and areas for development with regards to Emotional Intelligence.

Figure 11.1 **The Illness/Wellness Continuum**—Adapted from John Travis, 1988

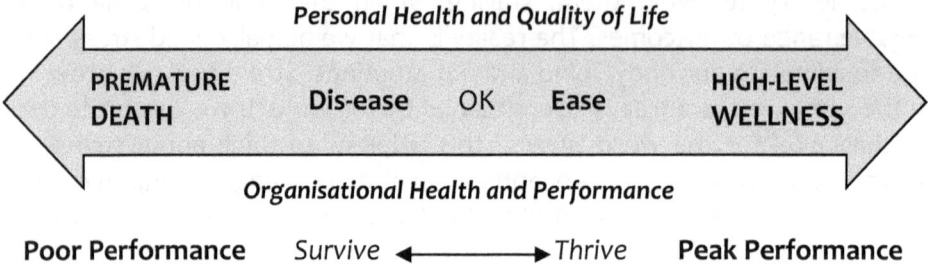

Living your Best Life

'Standard of living' is often confused with 'quality of life'. If we have to sacrifice our quality of life to maintain a high standard of living, (eg the latest car, house, and IPhone) we may lose ourselves and our most treasured relationships in the process.

When we are stressed, out of balance, living an unhealthy or unsustainable lifestyle, we are more likely to experience a lack of ease, with subsequent signs and symptoms of 'dis-ease' leading to illness in the long run.

Even if we are not obviously sick, we can still be unhappy, ill-at-ease, stressed or producing mediocre results in our life. In this 'OK Zone' we may occasionally experience peaks of wellness and bouts of illness as we go in and out of balance in our life, but for the most part we are only surviving, not thriving.

Wellness on the other hand, is usually achieved by those who live in alignment with their values, purpose, dreams, and their authentic self. Those who take care of their body, mind and soul, who take time to re-balance, to enjoy their passions and maintain healthy and fulfilling relationships, will experience higher levels of sustained wellness. High Level Wellness is characterised by higher levels of energy, resilience, happiness, fulfilment and contentment.

Figure 32.2 **The Balance Zone**—W Enright © 2005

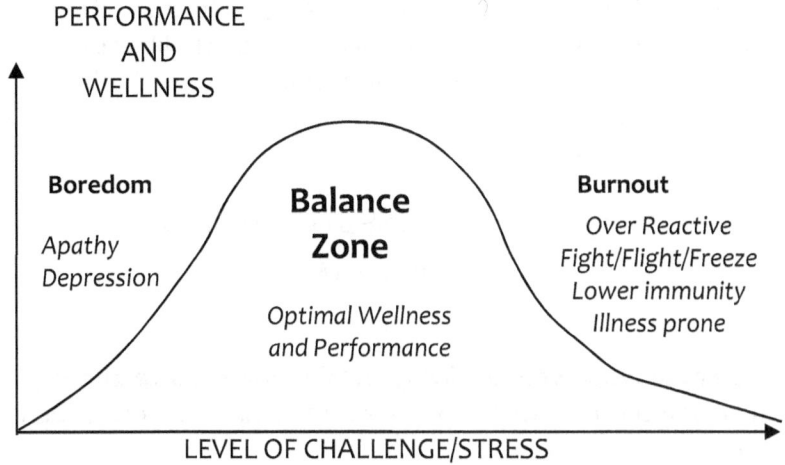

Surfing the Balance Zone
There is a fine line between stress and success depending on the level of challenge we face and our ability to respond it. To use a surfing analogy, we need a certain level of challenge (sizeable waves) to make life interesting but if we don't make any commitment, the waves will pass us by and we will eventually become bored, frustrated or disinterested in life. On the other hand if we paddle on to a wave and it picks up too much momentum and dumps us, we can wipeout. So, the key is to develop enough skill (mental and physical) to handle the waves and to only tackle those that we know we can handle or that stretch us enough to learn and improve, without wiping out too severely. As we tackle more challenging waves and develop our skills and confidence, our comfort zone expands and we can handle more.

As illustrated in Figure 32.2, there is an optimum level of challenge for each of us, where our quality of life and performance rises. If the level of challenge is too high or too low, these things deteriorate. As we expand our ability to respond to challenges, our comfort zone expands. Maintaining a balance between boredom and burnout is a continuous learning process. We are most well and perform at our best when we're in the Balance Zone.

The Gift of Illness

The gift of illness is often to re-balance us or teach us valuable lessons. Illness can therefore be a barometer—a red flag, urging us to treat ourselves more lovingly or to explore ways of healing the dis-ease we feel. Illness can therefore be viewed as a gift that provides valuable feedback. If we don't listen to the feedback, and the red flags go unheeded, this can sometimes lead to chronic illness or premature death.

Love your disease, it's keeping you healthy.
Dr John Harrison MD

How do you know when you are living outside the balance zone? (what are your most common red flags: physical, mental, emotional, behavioural symptoms?)

What are some things you can do when you notice your red flags beginning to surface (before they take hold completely), **so that you can restore balance?**

What can you do to help you maximise time in the balance zone and prevent boredom or burnout?

Surviving to Thriving
Abraham Maslow's Theory of Human Motivation (1943), expressed in his Needs Hierarchy Model (Figure 23.1)

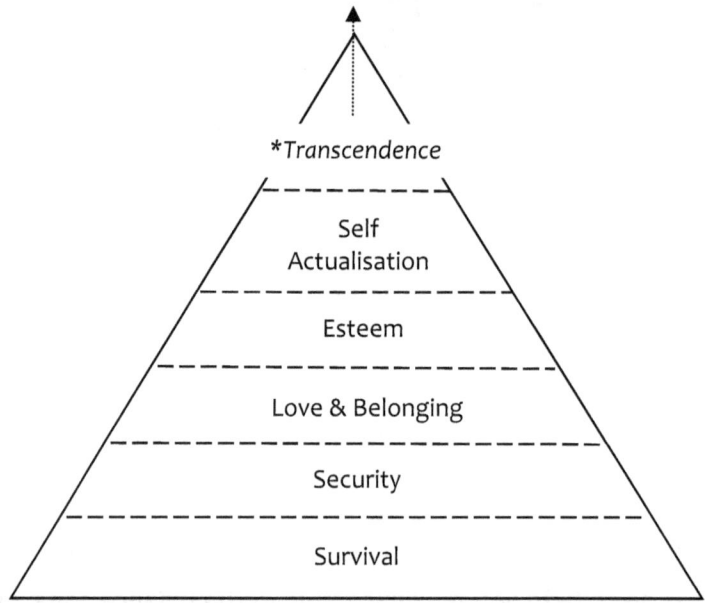

Abraham Maslow's theory of Human Motivation suggests that the most primary needs for human beings are survival and security, followed by love, approval and belonging, which provide a foundation for healthy self-esteem. Typically young people starting out in life, will have a higher level of self-esteem once they find reliable and meaningful employment and establish secure and loving relationships within a 'tribe' of like-minded friends.

Once these more primary needs are met consistently, we can focus more on what Maslow calls self-actualisation (achievement, becoming the best we can be). Concentration Camp survivor and Author of Man's Search for Meaning, Victor Frankl, added Transcendence as the 'pinnacle need' beyond self, which is about service to others and transcending worldly needs in the pursuit of meaning and spiritual growth.

When we act out of love rather than fear,
we can go from the security to surrender in an instant!

Progressing through these levels of Maslow's 'Needs Hierarchy' is not a once-off linear process—our needs oscillate daily and may regress during times of transition.

Interestingly, those who focus on personal growth and helping others, will often have their lower level needs met in the process. Finding True North and serving others, helps us to find meaning and purpose beyond our own self-serving needs.

What level of the Needs Hierarchy are you most focused on at this stage in your life?

What can you do to take care of your foundational needs, so that you can be happier, healthier and more fulfilled?

Transcendence and the Trans-personal
For many people, there is a sense of a greater presence, a force greater than ourselves, playing a part in the unfolding of our lives…and that they are contributing to something larger than their own lives…a greater meaning or spiritual dimension to their life.

This sense, which is more closely related to having faith in the unseen, or a trust in the bigger plan, can sometimes be significant enough to carry them through their more challenging times, as they reflect on major events, and begin to surrender the outcome of their actions realising that they cannot always be in control of that outcome.

This ability to surrender control of the outcome helps them to trust themselves more, and to have faith and peace that things will turn out ok in the end – even if it doesn't always look like that in the heat of the moment…this is called meaning-making, when people seek to makes sense of life events, relationships and the self… and is a key component of resilience.

Becoming involved in service clubs and volunteering can enhance this understanding, and taking time out to retreat from life and reflect from the grandstand either alone or with a mentor/guide can also assist. Meditation, mindfulness practices and prayer are also tools which enhance meaning-making.

Looking back on your life, describe some of the moments when you now realise that there was a greater 'plan' that you are a part of, which has helped to provided a sense of peace, knowing that you have done all you can do and can now surrender the outcome…?

_____
_____
_____
_____

Faith is taking the first step even when you don't see the whole staircase!
Martin Luther King

What are some actions that you can take or some practices that you can do, to remind you to stay more present to the knowledge that there is a spiritual growth dimension to your life's journey?

These actions/practices will help you to strengthen the foundations of who you are, stay connected to your True North and your passions, and thus live a more authentic and purpose-filled life, with greater resilience and response-ability.

Responsibility

Figure 33.1 **The Responsibility Model**—W Enright © 1991

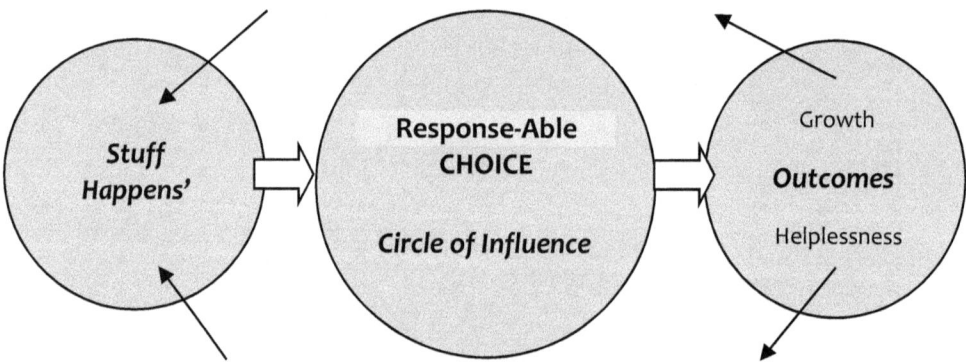

Responding to Change and Challenge

Response-Ability starts with our mental and emotional response to problems and crisis. Potentially stressful events can be considered 'good' or 'bad' depending on how we view them or how we choose to respond to them. At first, we may react without thinking but if we are mindful enough, we can cease reacting, step back from our circumstances and choose what we think, how we express our feelings and what we do to deal with our uninvited circumstances. We can become a master of our life circumstances, rather than giving our power away to them.

> *The secret to escaping the challenges of the world is
> to learn to love the world and all its challenges.*
>
> Ekart Tolle

The Mindfulness Paradox
Our ability to respond to life is significantly constrained or free, depending on how mindful we are. Being mindful is not a new concept; monks and meditators have been practicing it for thousands of years, although they would probably describe it as being 'Mind–Empty.' (ie less attached to our mind).

> *The beginner's mind sees many possibilities*
> *the expert's mind sees few.*
>
> Sogyal Rinpoche

Living in Present Time
Being mindful, simply means being more tuned into our present thoughts, feelings, body sensations, and our surrounding environment. Often we are so caught up in tasks, random thoughts and emotional reactions that we are not fully conscious of what we are doing, thinking and feeling. Our body, mind and emotions can end up dictating our enjoyment of life and our ability to deal with stress. Mindfulness helps us to live more in the moment with 'present time' awareness and without judgement (ie; without wishing it were otherwise).

When we are more mindful, we have a greater capacity to detach from stressful events. We can instead, observe them without attachment in much the same way as we observe passing traffic or a leaf floating down a stream. We are then in a better position to choose our response with greater awareness. Mindfulness is a psychological skill that can be mastered with practice first in easy situations then in more challenging circumstances.

Take a moment now to close your eyes and take a few deep, long breaths in and out, while you tune into all of your senses. What can you hear, smell, feel in your environment or in your body?

Figure 33.2 **Mindful Responsibility**

MINDFUL RESPONSIBILITY

Awareness
Be aware and mindful that this is an opportunity to practise and learn. You can choose your response.

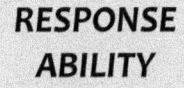
RESPONSE ABILITY

Evaluate Choices
After seeking to understand the situation & consulting your guiding principles, calmly evaluate your choices before taking decisive action.

Breathe
Slow, deep, relaxing breaths help you diffuse tension and respond mindfully without reacting.

Detach & Diffuse
Step back, detach and observe thoughts and feelings without judgement. Diffuse tension, fear & aggression. Calmly observe and listen before acting.

Calm
Calm yourself and others
Ask questions & empathise
Avoid pre-judging or over-reacting.

Reflect / Regroup
Take time out or away from the issue to reflect & regroup.

Release
If charged with emotion, take time to discharge it (Walk, talk, cry, change environment).

Breathe without Judgement
When we train ourselves to breath consciously, we are then more easily able to regulate our automatic 'fight/flight/freeze' reactions to challenging events. We may still experience fearful thoughts, unsettling feelings and stress, but we can observe them more calmly in the present moment, without judgement or attachment. Once we master this skill, we can then consider options and take decisive action from a place of conscious choice, rather than be reactive.

*Zen practice in the midst of activity
is superior to that pursued within tranquility.*

Hakuin

We can't always predict what the river and the ocean of life will do, but we can learn to read it somewhat and to improve our ability to respond mindfully. As we go through different stages in our life, the prevailing conditions change.
How do you regulate or express your emotional reactions in a crisis?

_____
_____
_____
_____
_____
_____
_____
_____

The 5 Pillars of Mindfulness

Breathe Consciously: The power of the Breath to transform our psycho-emotional state is incredible . . . take a deep breath, LET GO and BE CALM.

Be Present: Mono-tasking is the new black! Wherever you are . . . BE THERE . . . focus on the NOW.

Let go of Judgement: It is what it is! . . . letting go of judgement makes way for change, unity and open-mindedness to what may be unfolding . . . LET IT BE.

Have Gratitude: Appreciation of Beauty and Gratitude for what we already have helps our mind/body chemistry to shift from fear to PEACE.

Stay Hydrated: Hydration is vital to keep the brain active and 'switched on' throughout the day.

Set an intention to practise the 5 pillars daily.

Self Mastery and Life Balance

To sustain success in the public arena, we must first master ourselves in the way we manage our mind, body, emotions and spirit. People who are good self-managers have more energy, higher levels of wellness, and less stress. This state of being then helps them to perform at their optimum and to be a good role model for others. The resilience of a leader and their ability to respond to stress favourably, is significantly improved by sustaining a good life balance.

Figure 33.4 **The Life Balance Profile**—W&G Enright © 2005

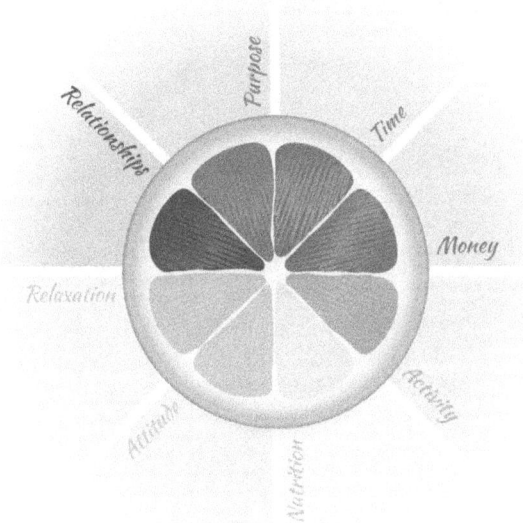

How Balanced are You?

Rate yourself on a scale from 1-10 for each of the areas of the Life Balance Profile? If the centre is zero and the outside edge of each spoke is 10, put a dot on the line to reflect your ratings. Then join the dots to see how well balanced your wheel is.

Achieving a 10 in each area is not necessarily the goal and is rarely sustainable. It is about being aware of when you are out of balance and knowing how to get back to your optimum level.

Energy Exchange

The flames between the circles of the True North Leadership compass symbolise the exchange of energy between us and those we interact with. Managing our own energy impacts our health, our ability to respond to life's challenges and the quality of our relationships with others.

In which areas of the Life Balance Profile are you most out of balance and what can you do to improve?

Influence

Earning the Right to Lead
People in positions of leadership are only supported by those who grant them the right to lead. This right must be earned through their daily actions, well chosen words and respectful relationships. When leaders are humble, empathic, trustworthy and respectful on a consistent basis, their ability to influence others is strengthened. To be trusted leaders need to be trust-worthy and to be respected they need to be respect-ful in their relations with others. There is a fine line between confidence and arrogance—it's called Humility.

*Self-confidence is a healthy strength to have
but few people respect arrogance.*

To live with true integrity, authenticity and mindfulness requires a willingness to be honest about our shortcomings and to live without pretense or false bravado. Humility engenders trust, empathy and respect. These are essential qualities for a leader, perhaps contrary to the belief that a leader must be strong, brave, courageous and unwavering in the face of adversity or personal fear and doubt. Through authentic speech, action and relationships, we earn the right to lead.

*Authentic leadership is not about position or title.
It is about being who you are with integrity and, through your honest actions,
words and relationships,
earning the right to lead.*

Figure 11.2 **Task/People Model**—Evolved from Mark Auricht, 1990

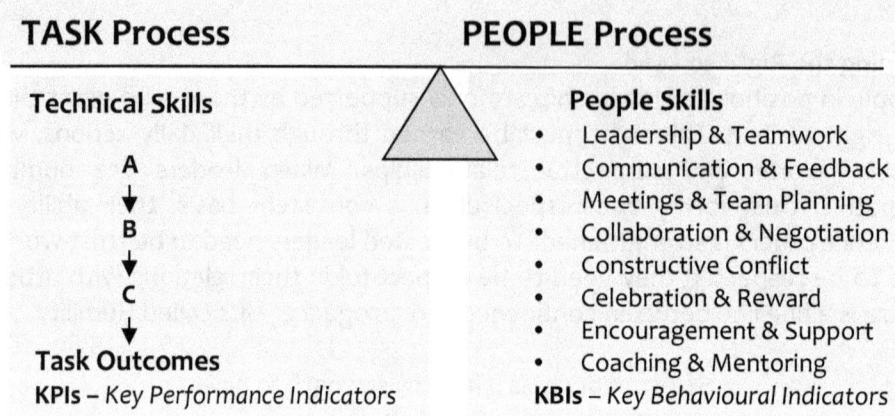

Social Intelligence – the art of dealing with people

The task side of the scale refers to the technical tasks involved in achieving outcomes. The people side of the scale refers to the people-processes involved in getting tasks done efficiently and effectively, thus leading to better performance outcomes, whether it be in a sports team, a family or a workplace team.

People skills, attitude and emotional intelligence far out-weigh intellect when it comes to leadership, teamwork and customer service.

Some trades and professions employ people based on their task competencies to begin with, but people skills and attitude will often be the deciding factor between two job candidates with the same technical qualifications.

Rate your ability to apply good people skills when you are under task pressure?

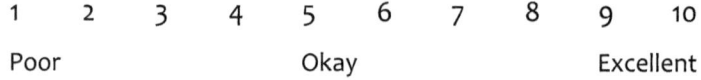

Identify the moments when your attention to task pressure has interfered with your people skills. What can you do to communicate more effectively with those around you at times like this?

Empathy and Diversity

Biological diversity is a core ingredient in the health of any eco-system, including human societies that are more likely to grow and thrive when diversity is embraced and used to advantage. At the same time, diversity does have its challenges when it results in prejudice and conflict. People differ in personality style, gender, culture, life experience, values, beliefs and priorities, so one of the biggest challenges for some people is to get along with people who are different to them.

Embracing differences doesn't mean that we need to agree with others who have a different point of view. However, it is helpful if we can seek to understand their perspective. Having empathy for others, no matter how different they are to us, helps us to build bridges of understanding that lead to less conflict and more co-operation. Sometimes we discover that we are not that different after all.

*A true practitioner of one religion
is a true follower of all religions.*

Gyuto Monks of Tibet

Understanding is more Important than Agreement
when we are dealing with someone we haven't gotten to know yet, or even when we are in a relationship with someone we like, it is common to have misunderstandings. Too much time and energy is wasted arguing for agreement or making stuff up because of a lack of communication. Understanding is more important than agreement.

The model below shows the inter-relationship between three things that contribute to the quality of relationship and understanding between people.

Figure 34.2 **Understanding Triangle** (Adapted ARC Triangle—Hubbard, 1950)

AFFINITY (Rapport)
1. Trust
2. Respect
3. Approachability
4. Connection

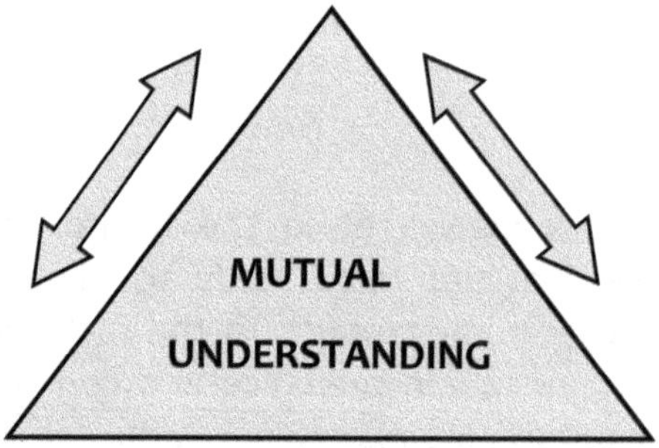

MUTUAL UNDERSTANDING

REALITY (Point of view)
1. On the same page
2. Alignment of vision/values
3. Shared perspective
4. Understanding each other's reality

COMMUNICATION
1. Empathy and Validation
2. Questioning
3. Listening
4. Clarifying

AFFINITY is the degree to which we feel aligned with each other and how much we like each other or have a rapport between us. Mutual respect and bridges of trust are key ingredients for strong affinity. Trust bridges sometimes take a long time to build. Weak trust bridges can break in an instant and are difficult to repair. Trust therefore, can be fragile or strong depending on the relationship. Affinity is built when we cross the trust bridge and know that it will be reliable.

What can you do to build greater trust with people in your key relationships?

....

....

....

....

....

....

REALITY is the point of view or perspective that each of us has. It includes the assumptions we make and our expectations and priorities. Our reality can sometimes be the same as another person but most often it will be different unless we can communicate clearly enough to clarify each other's point of view and come to some common understanding. Our challenge is to be able to acknowledge each other's truth without judgement. This is a choice available to all of us, to suspend judgement long enough to hear another's reality.

I can only say that I have come to know a truth, not the truth,
for truth has many faces.

COMMUNICATION is perhaps the most essential part of the Understanding Triangle, for without effective communication it is difficult to have mutual understanding of each other's reality or to have high levels of affinity. Asking questions to seek or clarify understanding, communicating with empathy and respect, giving feedback without invalidation; all of these aspects of communication contribute to mutual understanding and affinity.

Communication is the code that opens
the combination lock to understanding.

ARC Break
Whenever there is conflict or mis-understanding it is usually as a result of communication barriers, a difference in point of view or lack of affinity between people or groups. We call this an ARC Break. Like a break in a circuit, we can fix it by figuring out where the break is and doing our best to mend it. This often starts with communication, for example: expressing empathy; asking questions to seek understanding of the other's point of view; listening for their reality; clarifying assumptions; and acknowledging the other's perspective which helps to re-build rapport and trust. Once affinity is strengthened, the communication will usually start to flow and agreement/mutual understanding can be achieved. This becomes a self-reinforcing spiral.

Review a recent mis-understanding that you have had with someone. Viewed through the ARC lens, where do you feel the mis-understanding had its source?

_____

_____

_____

_____

_____

What could you have done differently to prevent or mend the ARC break?
(To minimise misunderstanding and build common ground more effectively)

_____

_____

_____

_____

_____

_____

Disagreement doesn't have to result in war.
If only we could sit around a fire, break bread, listen to each other's story
and choose to respect our differences.

Because we all have different personalities, different values and beliefs, different past experiences and points of view, it is not surprising that there will be an understanding gap between two or more people at any given time. Constructive conflict is based on the premise that everyone is right based on their perception and that the most constructive thing we can do is to seek understanding first and then move in the direction of a win-win if possible.

Constructive Conflict

When faced with a confrontation, an angry outburst or a difficult person, the key is to choose a constructive response rather than be sucked into matching the other person's behaviour, becoming defensive or going on the attack.

Figure 34.4 **Six Steps to Constructive Conflict**

SIX STEPS TO CONSTRUCTIVE CONFLICT

1. The first key skill is to remain calm and in control of your emotional response. If you can't do this, it might be best to take some time out before you are ready to respond. (Refer to Figure 33.2 Chapter 33.)

2. The second priority is to 'seek to understand' the other person by asking questions, acknowledging their feelings and listening to their point of view.

3. Check the accuracy of your understanding by reflecting back to the other person what you think they might be feeling and what you think they said. This demonstrates that you are listening and is much more powerful than just saying "I understand."

4. Never assume that the other person thinks the same way you do. Always ask questions and clarify before jumping to conclusions. Find out what their needs are and seek to fulfil them or at least acknowledge them. Be willing to co-operate.

5. Never blame, judge, criticise or demand. Always be calmly assertive, rather than aggressive. Use "I" statements to express how you feel, why you feel that way and what you'd prefer to happen now or next time.

6. Go for the win-win. Try to find some common ground or to figure out a way that both parties can benefit or at least feel that their point of view has been acknowledged and respected.

The impact of conflict only ends when there is forgiveness.
Letting go of attachment to hurt, heals us.

Non-judgement
We can improve our ability to regulate emotion in conflict situations by practicing the art of mindfulness. When we are more mindful, we have a greater capacity to detach, observe and respond from a place of considered choice because we have moderated our fight/flight response.

We are also less likely to be clouded by our assumptions and biases. We can instead, observe our reactions and the actions of others without attachment and judgement. It is also helpful to be conscious of our intentions, so that we are mindful of any hidden agendas we might have that cloud our judgement.

When we practice mindfulness, our ability to respond is set free, the boundaries we construct about the world and about ourselves and others, are more permeable or disintegrate altogether. Without these illusionary boundaries manufactured by the mind, we can see that we are all of equal value as human beings and have more compassion for each other. It is only the boundaries and limitations we put on ourselves and others that create inequality.

The Gift of Feedback
We can gain valuable insights from the feedback of others, if it is done with empathy, sensitivity and with the intention to help us improve. We can become aware of blindspots that might be hindering our performance or relationships. Constructive feedback delivered respectfully, helps us to become self-aware and to self-correct our behaviour without feeling invalidated. Feedback can be positive and affirming, as well as corrective.

6 Steps for Giving Feedback
1. Seek permission and appropriate time/place to give feedback.
2. Ask questions to seek understanding.
3. Actively listen to their reality.
4. Empathise with and acknowledge their point of view.
5. Give feedback about observed behaviour (blindspots)
6. Provide some guidance and encourage the person to improve.

It is important to put connection before correction

Think of someone you'd like to give some feedback to. What words will you use and in what order – to be as constructive as possible? (What non-verbal factors would also be helpful to be mindful of?)

Forgiveness is unlocking the door to set someone free and realising you were the prisoner!

Max Lucado

Embracing Differences
We are all have different personality traits. This diversity is an important strength in any team, family or community, bringing with it a good mix of different ways of thinking, doing and being. It can also be a source of conflict. Being self-aware with regard to our own personality preferences and embracing of differences in others, is helpful for building and maintaining healthy relationships.

Complete the 'Animal Instincts Profile' in the Appendix 1 to find out your personality type and tendencies.

Figure 34.7 **Animal Instincts** —W&G Enright © 2005

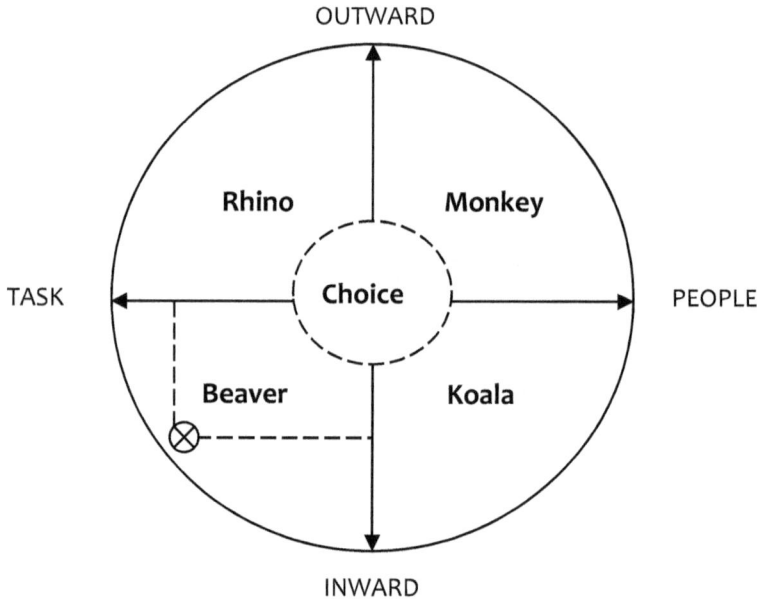

Figure 34.8 **Animal Instincts Table of Tendencies**—W&G Enright © 2005

Animal	RHINO	MONKEY	KOALA	BEAVER
Strengths	Decisive Achiever Focused Determined	People focus Creative Influence Fun	Empathy Support Calm Considerate	Details Structure Organisation Accuracy
Challenges	Too fast Low empathy	Miss detail Lack focus	Sensitivity Self-neglect	Perfectionist Being rushed
Stress Response	Bull dozer Force v Think	Humour Distraction	Withdraw Avoidance	Overwhelm OCD
Greatest Need	Respect In charge	Fun Attention	Peace Stability	Order Detail

It is useful to be aware of our strengths and weaknesses and to be able to modify our behaviour to suit the situation or the person we are needing to relate to. With practice and more mindful intention we can improve our ability to relate to people who may have the opposite tendencies to us. We are after all, a combination of all types which are simply a set of naturally preferred behaviours that can be regulated.

The key thing to be aware of is that everyone is different and we all have strengths. At the same time differences can cause conflict if we are not prepared to be flexible or to seek to understand each other and embrace our different communication styles. Leaders need to be acutely aware of this.

Individuals who live in alignment with their strengths and passions
are more fulfilled than those who are restrained by
the pots we put them in.

What is your predominant temperament and which of the personality Animals do you find most challenging to deal with?

Which of your strengths do you need to be most mindful of moderating so that it doesn't become too extreme?

The Ripple Effect

The final part of the True North Leadership Compass, is the outer circumference which is made up of a number of smaller circles which represent the people we influence in our lives. Just as the circles around the centre spiral represent the people, places and events that influence our leadership journey, so too do we become one of those circles for the people we influence.

This ripple effect is something that can happen by accident or by intention. Our influence continues to ripple out in ever widening circles to the edges of our circle of influence and beyond. This represents our legacy.

Our intentions, actions and words create a ripple effect that leaves a legacy, the impact of which we will never be fully aware, but which will continue on without us to the distant shores of the future.

> *The key to immortality*
> *is to live a life worth remembering*
>
> Bruce Lee

If your walk across life's shore were to make a difference in some way, what treasures would your footprints leave behind? (What legacy would you like to be remembered for?)

The Myth of Self-Mastery

Before we can have a significant influence in our external environment, we most often need to take a journey inward and learn to master ourselves first. The ripple effect of our commitment to personal growth cannot be underestimated. One small change inside a person can one day change the world.

Self-mastery, like life balance is perhaps an ideal to strive for but a reality that requires constant adjustment to the ever-changing matrix of life. When we see a person standing on one leg in a perfect yoga pose or karate stance, it looks like they are perfectly still but the truth is that the muscles of the leg and core are constantly making micro-adjustments to maintain the balance. Perhaps self-mastery is either a myth or a moment to moment proposition?

> *After all of our exploring,*
> *we arrive back where we began*
> *knowing ourselves for the first time.*
>
> TS Elliot

We never really arrive at the destination of ultimate self-mastery and have it stay done. Mastery is an ongoing process of practice, learning, self-discipline and growth. One only becomes a Black Belt for a moment and must then continue to practice daily to maintain and improve their skills and most importantly their attitude and approach to life.

If we want to achieve at least some level of self-mastery, we must first begin to master the ability to live more consciously.
Living more proactively sometimes requires us to question these habitual ways of living.

> *We either step forward into growth or back into safety.*
>
> Abraham Maslow

Understanding our ingrained patterns of behaviour and how to change them, often requires us to look a little deeper, to explore the thoughts, emotions and beliefs that support these habits. Our inner landscape needs to change before changes in our outer world will be sustainable.

Figure 35.1 **The Iceberg Model**—Adapted from Travis and Ryan, 1988

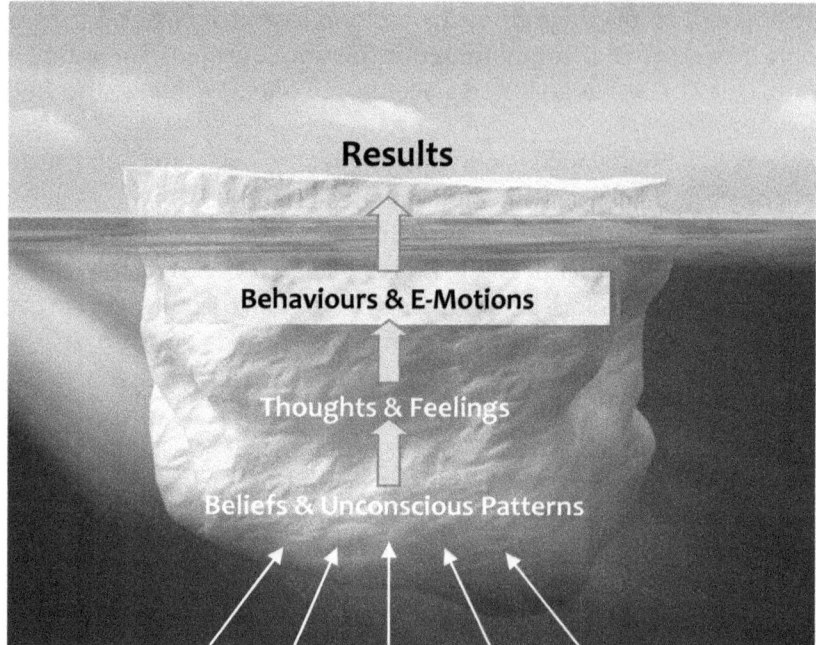

Our experiences influence the INNER RULES that we live by

The results we get in life, whether they be in the area of our health, relationships, work or community; are generally highly dependent on our behaviour, which is inexplicably linked to our mind, heart and soul. This can be represented by the metaphor of the iceberg where the results observed at the surface are supported by what lies beneath.

*If we want to change our outer world
we must first explore our inner landscape.*

Challenging the Inner Rules
Understanding what lies beneath the surface is the first step in mastering oneself or at the very least, mastering the process of changing behaviour so that we can move in the direction of wellness, improved performance and an optimum quality of life.

Our thoughts and feelings may be somewhat part of our natural make-up but tend to be programmed by our life experiences which influence the 'inner rules' that we live by. These 'inner rules' are the subconscious beliefs and conditioned response patterns that run our thoughts, feelings and behaviours—all of which extend from the bottom of this metaphorical iceberg to the surface of our life. We can try to make cosmetic changes to the tip of the iceberg but unless we start with re-programming the lower realms of the iceberg, any changes we make at the surface will be difficult to sustain for very long. If you chop off the top of an iceberg, the submerged part of the iceberg will pop up to the surface. This is a force of nature not to be denied and is as true for our health, as it is for our performance at work, or in our relationships at home.

From Story to Possibility
Our Inner Rules are significantly influenced by our 'Story.' The story we tell ourselves about who we are, what we're capable of, how much we are worth, what our strengths and weaknesses are. Reflecting on our 'Spiral Journey' can help us take an objective look at our Story and how it has influenced our self-talk, self-image, efficacy and esteem. This helps us to see where we have attached meaning to events and made subconscious decisions about how to respond to them. These may have helped us to cope in the past but may no longer be valid or constructive in our life now.

In each of us there is a potential waiting patiently for us to discover it. Sometimes even when it reaches out to us, saying "here I am", we miss the chance to bring it out of the shadows and into the light. Stretching to the outer reaches of our perceived boundaries is where we free ourselves from the shadows of our past.

> *"Life is not only a process of discovery,*
> *but also a process of creation.*
> *Seek therefore, to not only discover your hidden treasures but also to create who you want to be,*
> *by becoming the author of your life."*
>
> Adapted from a quote by Neale Donald Walsch
> Conversations with God

Fear Guards our Most Valuable Treasure

> *"Our deepest fears are like dragons*
> *guarding our deepest treasure"*
>
> Rainer Maria Rilk - Letters to a Young Poet

Fear is the greatest obstacle to achieving our potential and yet most fear is self-imposed, robbing us of our most valuable life experiences and opportunities to learn and become the best we can be. Like a bird in a cage with the door open, we can be imprisoned by our fear, not realising that we have the power to fly to our freedom. We can either stay in fear's cage or choose to fly free of it. A life lived in fear is a life half-lived. Living life adventurously is not about ignoring fear; it is about feeling it, facing it and pushing one's boundaries in spite of it, not in a reckless manner, but with courage and mindful responsibility.

Sometimes we must face our fears and venture into the high-country of the soul to find the truth of who we are and what we are capable of. On the other side of our fear is the freedom to be all that we can be. Resilience, responsibility and risk-taking are as important, if not more so, than the 3Rs we learn in school.

> *"Security does not exist in nature.*
> *Avoiding danger is no safer in the long run*
> *than outright exposure.*
> *Life is either a daring adventure or nothing."*
>
> Helen Keller

The Risk of Freedom

To express your dreams and ideals to the world is to risk ridicule.

To reach out to others is to risk commitment.

To love is to risk being vulnerable.

To hope is to risk disappointment.

To expose your emotions is to risk revealing your true heart.

To attempt success is to risk failure.

To live in full colour is to risk dying in the darkness.

Despite all of this, we must take risks, for the greatest tragedy in life is to risk nothing at all.

Those who avoid risk may minimise pain and penalty, but they simply cannot learn, feel, change, grow, love or live to their full potential.

Restrained by their fear, they become a prisoner, forfeiting their freedom.

Only those who are willing to risk can be truly free.

Adapted by WB Enright,
from a poem by William Arthur Ward (1921-1994)

For too long I'd been playing someone else's game. A game that took me away from what was important and required me to play by rules I didn't want to live by. I squandered time for the ones I loved and missed the beauty in the red, green and blue of our planet. In this place, among these people, I have re-discovered the joy of play, the beauty in nature and the balance that comes with rest and reflection.

When the Spirit of Adventure calls to your heart, may you remember without reservation, that you too can choose to follow it rather than fear it. Freedom is waiting.

Appendices

1. Animal Instincts profile
2. Emotional Intelligence Profile
3. Intention and Commitments
4. Circle of Stones
5. Dream Arrow
6. Creed Beads
7. Vision Board
8. Gratitude List

Appendix 1

Animal Instincts Profile

Please rate yourself on a **scale from 1 – 10**
to indicate how you see yourself most of the time, in most situations.

1 = not like me   5 = sometimes like me   10 = very much like me

1. Nurturing
2. Supportive
3. Sensitive
4. Encouraging
5. More passive
6. Rather listen than talk
7. Take time to make decisions.
8. Peacemaker
9. Empathic
10. Quietly spoken
11. Analytical
12. Organised
13. Good planner
14. Attention to detail
15. 'Perfectionist' streak
16. Tidy
17. Like structure
18. Like to think things through.
19. Decisions based on logic rather than emotion.
20. Prefer to work alone
21. Fun loving
22. Talkative
23. Animated
24. Highly spirited
25. Like attention
26. Energetic
27. Not into details
28. Focused on people before tasks.
29. Spontaneous
30. Don't like to be too structured
31. Driven
32. Like to get things done
33. Demanding of myself and others
34. Focused
35. Strong willed
36. Like to be in charge, rather than follow.
37. More fast paced
38. Like to be right
39. Like to do things my own way.
40. Have a competitive streak

Add totals for each group of questions below

ANIMAL	RELATED QUESTIONS	TOTAL SCORES FOR EACH
Koala	1 – 10	
Beaver	11 – 20	
Monkey	21 – 30	
Rhino	31 – 40	

Please note: This self-assessment and the *AI Table of Tendencies*[74] (Chapter 34), was developed by W Enright based on practical experience, and the work of Galenus, Marston and Hunt.

Appendix 2

Emotional Intelligence Profile

Rate yourself on a scale from 1 – 10 for each of the three aspects related to the five competencies. A rating toward the lower end of the scale means that you see yourself as deficient in this competency and need to significantly improve. A rating toward the upper end of the scale means that you see this trait as a strength of yours and would say that you feel quite competent in this area.

Self-Awareness
- Ability to tune into your feelings and use them to guide decisions [ ]
- A realistic assessment of your strengths and development needs [ ]
- A well-grounded sense of self-confidence [ ]

Self-Regulation
- Ability to handle your emotions under pressure [ ]
- Being able to handle ambiguity and uncertainty [ ]
- Recover well from emotional distress and disappointment [ ]

Motivation
- A strong drive to do what it takes to succeed [ ]
- Ability to persevere in the face of setbacks and frustration [ ]
- Optimistic attitude even when there are challenges to overcome [ ]

Empathy
- Having sensitivity for the feelings of others [ ]
- Ability to build rapport with a broad diversity of people [ ]
- Willingness to seek understanding & see things from another's perspective [ ]

Social Skills
- Skill in managing relationships and building connections [ ]
- Being able to negotiate and settle disputes or disagreements [ ]
- Ability to influence and lead others [ ]

Notes: Adding scores for the three aspects within each competency will give you a combined score for that competency. Competencies with a combined score higher than 20 are considered a strength. A total score of 100+, after aggregating all five competencies, indicates a 'healthy' level of Emotional Intelligence. Emotional competencies tend to increase as one matures with life experience. Emotional development can be accelerated by taking risks and expanding one's comfort zone.

Please note: This self-assessment was developed by W Enright based on the 5 Competencies outlined by Daniel Goleman in his book: *Working with Emotional Intelligence* (see References).

Appendix 3

Intention and Commitments

Use this template to set and commit to your intentions

Specific
Describe specifically what it is you would like to do or achieve. Be specific about the action steps you need to take.

Action 1.   When:

Action 2.   When:

Action 3.   When:

Measurable
How will you measure your success / what will be the reward?

Measure: Reward:

Achievable
Set goals that stretch you and that are realistically achievable. If your goal is too big break it down into achievable chunks.

First step:

Responsible
Who can you make a commitment to and who can help to motivate and support you?

Who:

Time defined.
When will you take the action specified above and on what date would you like to complete your goal. **Date:** _____

Appendix 4

Circle of Stones

It is October 2012 and I find myself alone in a remote area of the Northern Flinders Ranges, sitting in the red dust under a blanket of black between the stars. I feel the dark chill of the night and sense the nocturnal beings watching me as I sit on the earth surrounded by a circle of stones... listening to the silence of the present while reflecting on the tracks of my past.

I have been alone now for 3 days and nights, just me, the wilderness and the raw reality of my body, mind and emotions. No music, books, people, time piece or food to distract me from myself. Only 12 litres of water and a tarp for shelter from the rain and sun, should I choose to escape their intensity.

This is the last night of 'Solo Time' on my Vision Quest. During this time I have been reflecting on my past and my future, keeping a journal, going for short walks in the cool of the morning and climbing some rocky outcrops at dusk to survey the view.

Solitude is the place of purification.

On this last night before returning to a distant base camp to share my story, I am completing a ritual called the 'Circle of Stones,' where one chooses a number of rocks or stones to represent people, places or events in one's life that have had an impact or perhaps represent some unfinished business. This is an opportunity to see the path we have taken, the choices we have made, the people, places and events that have shaped us and to express gratitude, forgiveness or acknowledgement.

I have placed the rocks in a circle about 4 metres in diameter. At sunset I closed the circle with one last rock, making a commitment to stay within the circle until sunrise. I sacrifice sleep for quiet reflection while I take a nostalgic and sometimes confronting journey around my 'Circle of Stones.' During this night I have contemplated quietly, laughed loudly and cried with joy, rage, grief and gratitude. I have written letters to the living and the dead or the words left unsaid. Among all of these things I have found peace and clarity.

For the last time this night I look at the moon as it creeps along its arc through the night sky towards the horizon in the west. Not wearing a watch, I imagine the increments of time that have passed from sunset through to now. I sense that it's about "that it's about half an hour before first light. As if on cue, I hear in the distance, the melodic song of a solitary bird searching for the dawn… that beautiful whistle one hears just before sunrise.

I only have a little while to go now before the sun comes up, then I will remove the most eastern stone from the circle and through this gate I will walk towards the sunrise of my future, taking with me the treasure from my past.

Among the foundation stones of our life we find gems of immeasurable value. I asked myself that night: Shall I leave them hidden in the dust of my past or reveal the beautiful light reflected through them for all to see?

Solitude
When we spend time alone, our fears and doubts come to the surface. Like a wise artisan, solitude carves away at our façade, revealing our authentic self, helping us to confront our weaknesses and embrace our strengths. Without distraction, we see things as they are and we have time to contemplate truth and illusion. Time for reflection is a precious gift that can provide many blessings if we have the courage to see, to hear and to act on the truth we discover in silence.

> *Solitude is where we learn, what we can only learn alone.*
> *When we return, we can then share the gift of our learning*
> *for the benefit of others.*

Sacred Stones Activity
Consult your notes on the people, places and events in your life that you'd like to acknowledge, complete unfinished business with, honour, forgive or simply express gratitude for. Choose some stones to represent these and spend some time alone inside the circle of stones.

Be present with each stone, sitting/standing face on.

Silently/out loud, you may wish to dialogue, and listen with your inner ear to the messages and insights these people, places and event may have for you. Jot down any significant information. Conclude your process with honour, gratitude and forgiveness where appropriate.

Appendix 5

Dream Arrow

A dream arrow is a metaphor that represents the act of fashioning your dreams into a life and launching it forward into the future.

Find a piece of driftwood, a dead fallen branch from a tree that is not being used as habitat by any animal, or a stick that you've purchased or found in some place special.

Take time to carve or sand the wood to your liking. Then decorate it with coloured string, feathers or beads.

Write 10 dreams on small pieces of paper – choose things from your Have, Do, Give, Be lists that you would like to manifest in the future. **Tie these dreams to your arrow and hang it somewhere special.**

In 10 years, open up the pieces of paper and see how many of your dreams have come true.

Appendix 6

Creed Beads

Creed beads are a symbol of your values to remind you of your creed.

Using a long piece of leather and some wooden beads of different shapes and colours, make a bracelet or necklace.

Each bead represents one of your key values or character traits you see as important to who you are.

Eg; Learning, balance, health, compassion, courage etc.

Appendix 7

Vision Board

A vision board will help you to visualise the things, qualities, experiences, people, that you would like to attract into your life or focus on creating.

Collect some magazines about topics that interest you. For example – travel, outdoors, homes, family, boats, cars, sport, gardens, wellness, spirit, camping, education, etc

Then find a relaxed place with some music, wine, food, candles – whatever makes you relaxed and creative.

Without thinking too much flip through the magazines and cut out any pictures or words that you resonate with.

Using your intuition, stick all the pieces on a large piece of colour card to create a vision of the future you desire.

Appendix 8

Gratitude List

Sometimes we easily forget all of the blessings in our life – our health, our relationships, the experiences we have had, the lessons we have learned, the things that are going well for us, the challenges that have made us stronger and the simple things that we take for granted.

Make a list of all the things, people, places, events and conditions of your life that you are grateful for. Focusing on gratitude every day, keeps our mind, heart and spirit healthy. This inevitably flows over into our physical well being and our relationships with others.

You may choose to dedicate a specific journal to this practice on a daily basis, identifying 3 things each day you are grateful for.

Honouring Truth

*A truth once experienced, changes our trajectory.
Like one atom colliding innocently with another,
changing our course forever.*

*We honour this truth
in the way we live our lives thereafter.*

To provide feedback or to order copies of the book:

The Spirit of Adventure Calls: A Compass for Life Learning & Leadership,
Please contact wayne@freespirittruenorth.com.au

Wayne and Gabrielle Enright are facilitators of Personal Development journeys specialising in Adventure, Leadership and Wellbeing.

For more information please visit www.freespirittruenorth.com.au